Poems From South Wales Vol II

Edited by Heather Killingray

First published in Great Britain in 2006 by:
Young Writers
Remus House
Coltsfoot Drive
Peterborough
PE2 9JX
Telephone: 01733 890066
Website: www.youngwriters.co.uk

SB ISBN 1 84602 602 4

Foreword

Young Writers was established in 1991 and has been passionately devoted to the promotion of reading and writing in children and young adults ever since. The quest continues today. Young Writers remains as committed to the nurturing of poetic and literary talent as ever.

This year's Young Writers competition has proven as vibrant and dynamic as ever and we are delighted to present a showcase of the best poetry from across the UK and in some cases overseas. Each poem has been selected from a wealth of *A Pocketful Of Rhyme* entries before ultimately being published in this, our fourteenth primary school poetry series.

Once again, we have been supremely impressed by the overall quality of the entries we have received. The imagination, energy and creativity which has gone into each young writer's entry made choosing the poems a challenging and often difficult but ultimately hugely rewarding task - the general high standard of the work submitted ensured this opportunity to bring their poetry to a larger appreciative audience.

We sincerely hope you are pleased with this final collection and that you will enjoy *A Pocketful Of Rhyme Poems From South Wales Vol II* for many years to come.

Contents

The Poems

My Week In Colour

On Monday I felt blue because
I was cold and it was wet.

On Tuesday I felt yellow because
I was really happy and it was sunny not gloomy.

On Wednesday I felt green because
I was ill, but just faking.

On Thursday I felt white because
I was calm, my mind was clear,
instead of loads of memories.

On Friday I felt black because
I was scared of my maths test.

On Saturday I felt grey because
I felt miserable and sad.

On Sunday I felt gold because
I was clean, I had to go to church.

Daniel Christopher (9)
Abernant Primary School, Aberdare

My Week In Colour

On Monday I felt yellow because I was happy
when I saw all my friends in school.
On Tuesday I felt green because Courtney lent Alex a pen and not me.
On Wednesday I felt grey because it was cloudy and raining.
On Thursday I felt purple because I was embarrassed
when everyone had their homework and not me.
On Friday I felt red because I was angry when the boys
wouldn't let me play.
On Saturday I felt blue because I was calm riding my horse.
On Sunday I felt white because I felt ill and scared.

Alesha Sandor (9)
Abernant Primary School, Aberdare

My Week In Colour

On Monday I felt red because I forgot my
homework and I was scared.

On Tuesday I felt yellow because the sun
was shining and I was playing.

On Wednesday I felt white because
I forgot my homework.

On Thursday I felt blue because
this girl had something I wanted.

On Friday I felt green because
I was sick.

On Saturday I felt grey because
I was miserable like my mam.

On Sunday I felt orange because
it was warm and I was happy.

Aimee Evans (9)
Abernant Primary School, Aberdare

My Week In Colour

On Monday I felt grey because it was miserable
and it was back to school.
On Tuesday I felt white because I was ill.
On Wednesday I felt black because I was frightened
because I lost my homework.
On Thursday I felt yellow because I was happy the sun was shining.
On Friday I felt purple because I was embarrassed by the test.
On Saturday I felt red because I was hot, I did squash.
On Sunday I felt blue when I went to church and it was cool.

Martha Makin (6)
Abernant Primary School, Aberdare

My Week In Colour

On Monday I felt yellow because
I was happy it was sunny.

On Tuesday I felt blue because
I was cold and it was windy.

On Wednesday I felt green
when I was ill after eating nuts.

On Thursday I felt red when I was
hurt when I cut myself.

On Friday I felt grey because
I was miserable when it was raining.

On Saturday I felt orange because
it was sunny.

On Sunday I felt black because
I was sad when it was pouring.

Jac Cooper (8)
Abernant Primary School, Aberdare

My Week In Colour

On Monday I felt blue because I felt very calm.
On Tuesday I felt grey because it was tipping down with rain.
On Wednesday I felt green because I was very ill
and I was in bed all day.
On Thursday I felt red because I was angry when Mam said
we couldn't go bowling.
On Friday I felt yellow because it was a lovely, nice, hot day.
On Saturday I felt white because I was scared of rugby
and it was a big, big game for us to win.
On Sunday I felt purple because I was miserable
as we lost the football game.

Gabriel Williams (9)
Abernant Primary School, Aberdare

My Week In Colour

On Monday I felt red because the heaters would not turn off
and I was hot.
On Tuesday I felt blue because the central heating had broken
and I was cold.
On Wednesday I felt black because nobody wanted to play
and I was sad.
On Thursday I felt white because there was no electricity
and I was scared.
On Friday I felt yellow because the sun was out all day
and I was happy.
On Saturday I felt green because my brother had one pound
and I was jealous.
On Sunday I felt grey because my bed broke and collapsed
and I was miserable.

Benjamin Thomas (8)
Abernant Primary School, Aberdare

My Week In Colour

On Monday I felt red because I was angry that my sister
hid my pretend sword.
On Tuesday I felt blue because I went swimming in the water.
On Wednesday I felt pink because I was embarrassed
when I slept in my sister's bed.
On Thursday I felt green because we were eating at the table
and after my sister could have sweets and I could not.
On Friday I felt yellow because I went to my friend's house
and I played on his Xbox.
On Saturday I felt orange because we had a big fire.
On Sunday I felt black because I slept in the dark
and my father scared me all the time.

Thomas Mason (8)
Abernant Primary School, Aberdare

My Week In Colour

On Monday I felt green because I was jealous,
Year 5 and 6 were going to Saint Fagon's and my class hadn't gone.

On Tuesday I felt blue because I was cold
as my heater had broken.

On Wednesday I felt white because I was ill and
had been sick and I was as white as a sheet.

On Thursday I felt black because I was scared that
my teacher would give me a row for not doing my homework.

On Friday I felt yellow because there was no school
for six weeks and we had no homework.

On Saturday I felt grey because it was raining,
thundering and lightning, it was a miserable day.

On Sunday I felt red because it was boiling and I was happy
it was like a summer's day, the sun was out and I could go out
to play and see my friends.

Alice Israel (8)
Abernant Primary School, Aberdare

My Week In Colour

On Monday I felt blue because I was freezing cold.
On Tuesday I felt red because I was boiling hot.
On Wednesday I felt green because I was jealous that my brother
didn't have homework but I did.
On Thursday I felt yellow because we were going swimming
and I was happy.
On Friday I felt white because I was scared of doing my maths
and English test.
On Saturday I felt black because I was sad when I fell off my bike.
On Sunday I felt grey because I was scared that I might forget
my homework for Mrs Jones to mark.

Rhiannon Davies (8)
Abernant Primary School, Aberdare

My Week In Colour

On Monday I felt red because
I wanted to go on the school trip and I couldn't.

On Tuesday I felt white because
I forgot to do my homework.

On Wednesday I felt gold because
I won the boys' skipping race.

On Thursday I felt purple because
I didn't do my work properly and felt embarrassed.

On Friday I felt grey because
It was a very miserable day and I couldn't go outside.

On Saturday I felt blue because
I was blue.

On Sunday I felt red with excitement because
I was going round my friend's house.

Oliver Pritchard (8)
Abernant Primary School, Aberdare

My Week In Colour

On Monday I felt red because we had to go to school.
On Tuesday I felt blue because it was cold and windy.
On Wednesday I felt white because I was ill - I had a cold and bad tum.
On Thursday I felt yellow because I was happy it was hot.
On Friday I felt grey because it was the maths test and spelling test.
On Saturday I felt green because my dad went to London and I didn't.
On Sunday I felt purple because I was embarrassed
when I spilt a drink on my dress in the shopping centre.

Hollie Davies (9)
Abernant Primary School, Aberdare

My Week In Colour

On Monday I felt yellow because it was a nice day
and it was the first day of school.

On Tuesday I felt dark red when someone stole my pen
so I could not use it.

On Wednesday I felt blue because I was going to have
English homework.

On Thursday I felt green because I was eating
a lot at dinner time.

On Friday I felt black because I forgot to
give my homework in.

On Saturday I felt purple when I fell and
I had cuts on my knees.

On Sunday I felt grey because it was raining
heavily on my house.

Katie Lloyd Jones (9)
Abernant Primary School, Aberdare

My Week In Colour

On Tuesday I felt white
because I didn't do my homework.
On Friday I felt green because
I was jealous as I wanted a phone like my sister's.
On Saturday I felt blue because
it was cold in the house.
On Sunday I felt orange because
it was warm.

Bethany Lloyd (9)
Abernant Primary School, Aberdare

My Week In Colour

On Monday I felt grey because it was miserable
and it was the first day of school.

On Tuesday I felt red with love
when my boyfriend kissed me!

On Wednesday I felt green with jealousy because
Year 3 got to go on the computer and Year 4 didn't.

On Thursday I felt pink because
my mother embarrassed me.

On Friday I felt black because I was
frightened and it was dictation.

On Saturday I felt yellow, I was happy
and it was the weekend.

On Sunday I felt blue with calmness
because I was meditating.

Alexandra Moore (9)
Abernant Primary School, Aberdare

My Week In Colour

On Monday I felt green because Miss Hartnell's class
went on a school trip and I was jealous.
On Tuesday I felt blue because it was wet and miserable
and I was very sad it was raining.
On Wednesday I felt white because I was upset,
I didn't like the cook's dinner.
On Thursday I felt yellow because the sun was
shining on me.
On Friday I felt purple because I was very happy.
On Saturday I felt black because I was frightened
when I lost my homework.
On Sunday I was red because I was full of love,
it was Valentine's Day.

Sarah Lloyd Jones (7)
Abernant Primary School, Aberdare

My Week In Colour

On Monday I felt red because I did not
remember my homework to bring to school for some more.

On Tuesday I felt blue because the heaters
were not working so we were very cold.

On Wednesday I felt yellow because Mrs Hartnell's class
went to Saint Fagan's and went out of school.

On Thursday I felt green because a different class
went to Saint Fagan's and went out of school.

On Friday I felt grey because it was raining heavily
so we couldn't go out to play.

On Saturday I felt black because I was scared that
Miss would mark our work.

On Sunday I felt white and was pale
because I was ill.

Katie Piggott (7)
Abernant Primary School, Aberdare

My Week In Colour

On Monday I felt blue because it rained all day through.
On Tuesday I felt yellow because the sun shone all day.
On Wednesday I felt green because I had a bug all day.
On Thursday I felt red because I was hot.
On Friday I felt purple because there was a maths test.
On Saturday I felt black because I scored nil in the maths test.
On Sunday I felt grey because there was school tomorrow.

Thomas Hunnisett (7)
Abernant Primary School, Aberdare

My Week In Colour

On Monday I felt yellow
because I was happy.

On Tuesday I felt white
because I was ill.

On Wednesday I felt red
because I saw a rose.

On Thursday I felt black
because I was sad.

On Friday I felt blue
because I was cold.

On Saturday I felt grey
because I was miserable.

On Sunday I felt green
because I was jealous.

Courtney Lacey (8)
Abernant Primary School, Aberdare

Autumn - Haiku

Leaves are on the ground
Twisting planes flying around
Orange and red fade.

Abigail Coombs (7)
Heol-y-Cyw Primary School, Bridgend

Winter - Haiku

The snow is falling
People are having snow fights
Children are quite cold.

Matthew Cox (7)
Heol-y-Cyw Primary School, Bridgend

Happiness

Happiness is like shining yellow stars,
It sounds like lively, joyful laughter,
It tastes like juicy, sticky sweets,
It looks like two gigantic bouncy balls,
It feels like pretty butterflies moving inside my tummy,
It reminds me of my funny, caring, happy friends.

Natasha Cox (9)
Heol-y-Cyw Primary School, Bridgend

Autumn - Haiku

Leaves are on the mud
Red leaves crashing to the ground
Brown and yellow fall.

Camaron Davies (7)
Heol-y-Cyw Primary School, Bridgend

Love

Love is the colour of warm shades of pink,
It sounds like romance and happiness,
Love tastes like chocolate with cold cream,
Love looks like beautiful love hearts,
Love feels like a soft, bouncy duvet,
Love reminds you of lovely times and lovely food.

Elli Beckinsale (8)
Heol-y-Cyw Primary School, Bridgend

Winter - Haiku

Snow comes down at night
The snowflakes are falling hard
The children have fun.

Rhys Jordan (6)
Heol-y-Cyw Primary School, Bridgend

Happiness

Happiness is a gold diamond,
It sounds like a beautiful bird tweeting,
It tastes like a sweet cup of tea,
It looks like a pink flamingo with a delicate neck,
It feels like a tiger's mane,
It reminds me of a whale jumping through the sea.

James Perry (9)
Heol-y-Cyw Primary School, Bridgend

Love

Love is bright pink like a love heart,
It sounds like quiet music,
It tastes like fruity sweets,
It looks like a squashy pillow,
It feels like a fluffy puppy,
It reminds me of my parents.

Jessica Perry (9)
Heol-y-Cyw Primary School, Bridgend

Love

Love is as red as a beautiful rose,
It sounds like slow romantic music,
It tastes like strawberries and cream,
It looks like a roaring fire,
It feels like the beating of a wonderful tambourine,
It reminds me of my lovely baby sister.

Ethan James (9)
Heol-y-Cyw Primary School, Bridgend

The Hunter Of The Sea

I am long, slim and gentle,
Blue or silver, two fins and one tail.
I am fast and swift, suddenly I appear
Suddenly I disappear.
I live in soft, gentle seas.
I squeak and chatter,
I swim and search
For tasty fishes.
Who am I?

Holly Isitt (10)
Pantysgallog Primary School, Dowlais

My Rainbow Poem

Red is for a Welsh dragon flapping his wings in the sky.
Orange is a sun made of a ball of fire.
Yellow is a daffodil moving side to side.
Green is for the grass and the leaves to make flowers grow.
Blue is for a snowflake drifting to the ground.
Indigo is for the deepest ocean swishing up and down.
Violet is for a pansy petal falling to the ground.

Jessica Leonard (10)
Pantysgallog Primary School, Dowlais

The Old Dog - Haiku

The little old dog,
Sitting on my rug resting,
Chewing on his bone.

Heather Magee (9)
Pantysgallog Primary School, Dowlais

My Hutch

I'm very smooth, I can also be cute,
sometimes grumpy and
I'm a mammal.
I have got a short tail, and big
ears and I've also got four feet.
I can be in
all colours but mostly brown or
black.
I'm very fast,
I also live in a hutch or in
a garden.
I come out in the spring,
biting the flowers.
The noise I make
is twitching my
nose and I eat
carrots and grass.
Who am I?

Lauren Jade Rees (9)
Pantysgallog Primary School, Dowlais

My Rainbow Poem

Red is a ruby on a shining golden ring.
Orange is a tangerine in a bowl of juicy fruit.
Yellow is a daffodil standing tall in a field.
Green is a lime filled with sour juice.
Blue is a stream running through the forest.
Indigo is the night sky with stars dotted around.
Violet is a hyacinth dancing in the field.

Kayleigh Mahoney (9)
Pantysgallog Primary School, Dowlais

A Lazy Animal

Tall and long am I.
I have patches of yellow-brown.
I am a fast animal
On my four long legs.
I live on grassland and eat from trees.
I *crunch, crunch* on leaves all day long.
I have a long neck that reaches the treetops.
What am I?

Tyler Cook (10)
Pantysgallog Primary School, Dowlais

The Small Animal

I am small and furry with legs.
I am grey and black with a long tail.
I scurry across the ground,
I live in a big barn.
I am squeaky all the time.
I nibble, I eat nuts
And I eat wheat for energy.
What am I?

Kelly Lewis (10)
Pantysgallog Primary School, Dowlais

Haiku

The sweet little girl
Ran around the park one day
With her skipping rope.

Lara Carroll
Pantysgallog Primary School, Dowlais

The Lizard - Haiku

The massive lizard
Lives in very hot jungles
Waiting for insects.

Lloyd Davies (10)
Pantysgallog Primary School, Dowlais

The Badger - Haiku

A giant badger
Is waiting in a burrow
For some juicy worms.

Kyle Howe (10)
Pantysgallog Primary School, Dowlais

German Shepherd

His fierce fighting teeth
And his fast running feet
Robbers run away.

Toby Bluck (9)
Pen-y-Fai CiW Primary School, Bridgend

Beagle - Haiku

The beagle waits still
Sniffs out its prey for its tea
Its prey doesn't know.

Ethan Candlish-Nott (9)
Pen-y-Fai CiW Primary School, Bridgend

Autumn's Come

There came a day when Autumn tucked Summer away
'Now what shall I do with the leaves?'
The day said, the day said,
'Make them brown, make them brown.
Let them go where they dare.'
'Now what shall I do with the colour?'
The day said, the day said,
'Make it dim, make it dim.'

Alex Campbell (8)
Pen-y-Fai CiW Primary School, Bridgend

Dolphins

Gliding dolphins in the sunset,
Swimming to their prey, the scaly fish,
Chew their prey and leave the blue skin,
Ocean swings, killing rocks,
Dolphins hide to sleep tonight,
Dolphins sleeping, fish swimming.
The sun sets, goodnight!

Leah Bassett (9)
Pen-y-Fai CiW Primary School, Bridgend

Summer Comes

Summer comes
    we'd better get our summer things out.
Summer comes
    we need to go swimming.
Summer comes
    I'm getting ready.
Summer comes
    we need suncream.
Summer comes
    I'm earning money.
Summer comes
    I'm going on holiday.
Summer comes
    I love the summer.

Ashley Jenkins (9)
Pen-y-Fai CiW Primary School, Bridgend

Tornado

The big black tornado
Spinning in the sun. What shall we do?
We'll take cover people.
Quickly, take tons of food to your shack.
You have to be safe.
I can feel it sucking up people,
Cars and trucks are crushed too!
Houses, cars, buses, trucks, what next?
Someone stop it, please! please!

Dafydd Jones (9)
Pen-y-Fai CiW Primary School, Bridgend

Guess Who?

Colourful thing
Loves to sing.

Flying around
Or sitting on the ground.

Eating a worm
That loves to squirm.

Making a nest
Is the best.

Leaves muck all around
But mostly on the ground.

Has a pointing beak
And sometimes squeaks.

What am I?
A: Bird.

Rebecca Smalley (9)
Pen-y-Fai CiW Primary School, Bridgend

Winter Wonderland And Spring Has Sprung

Skiing in the big, thick snow
Going round icy icicles
Chasing ducklings who do not know.

Leaves are falling on the ground
Children are playing all around
Spring is over, summer's come.

Toby-Michael Galliers (8)
Pen-y-Fai CiW Primary School, Bridgend

Guess What

Rolling in a ball
So, so small.

He's not fussed
Sleeping in sawdust.

Eating food
In a good mood.

Biting people he meets
When he's having treats.

In a cage
Gnawing with rage.

Making a mess
And giving you stress.

A: Hamster.

Chloe Osborn (9)
Pen-y-Fai CiW Primary School, Bridgend

Smelly Sammy

Smelly Sammy
Spent silly seconds
Singing slowly.
Smelly Sammy
Shrinks shirts.
Smelly Sammy
Slurps soup.
Sammy shops Saturday.
She sells sticky sweets.
She seriously stinks.

Victoria Leyshon (10)
Pen-y-Fai CiW Primary School, Bridgend

Guess What

Cold night
Frost bite.

Woolly hats
Freezing cats.

Cosy fire
Singing choir.

Icicles hanging
People banging.

Trees swaying
Children laying.

Cup of tea
Frozen key.

Chattering teeth
Falling leaves.

A: Winter.

Samantha Griffiths (8)
Pen-y-Fai CiW Primary School, Bridgend

I Like Cheese

I like cheese and crackers.
I like cheese and ham toasties.
I like cheese on toast.
I like cheese in a bun.
I like cheese in a sandwich.
I like cheese by itself.

I love cheese!

Daniel Newman (9)
Pen-y-Fai CiW Primary School, Bridgend

Guess Who

Rides a carriage
And her children are into marriage.

A hundred beads on her dress,
Or maybe less.

A good look in her eye,
Once she has to say goodbye.

This lady is getting old now,
And if you saw her you would have to take a bow.

She has four children and two corgi dogs,
Who like to lie out in the sunshine by some logs.

She is head of the Church of England,
And her many homes are very grand.

She lives in posh Buckingham Palace,
And we don't want to bear her any malice.

A: Elizabeth II.

Rebekah White (9)
Pen-y-Fai CiW Primary School, Bridgend

Great White Shark

There's a fast thing swimming around their boat
With big long things around the boat.

One diver dived in the water and he panicked
And he was in its mouth.

The people drove back to their homes
But the shark was chasing
And then it went away.

Callum Matthews (9)
Pen-y-Fai CiW Primary School, Bridgend

Guess What

Huge splasher
Silver basher.

Jumps high
Loves pie.

Keeps low
Wears a bow.

Good swimmer
Comes in winter.

Fast eater
Big beater.

In my bowl
Like my soul.

A: Fish.

Charlotte Price (10)
Pen-y-Fai CiW Primary School, Bridgend

Guess Who

Beer drinker
But brilliant thinker.

Goal scorer
Champagne pourer.

Good passer
Bad crosser.

Legendary forward
Never lowered.

Dead now
But how?

A: George Best

Marco Jones (9)
Pen-y-Fai CiW Primary School, Bridgend

Guess What

She's very sneaky
We see her weekly.

She's my pet
She's always wet.

She's very white
A bit too bright.

She loves to play
She sleeps in hay.

She loves water
She's like my daughter.

She likes food
But is very rude.

A: Rabbit.

Georgia Thomas (10)
Pen-y-Fai CiW Primary School, Bridgend

Guess What

Good diver
Underwater glider.

Shell snatcher
Fish catcher.

Fast swimmer
Water skimmer.

Bird seizer
Baby teaser.

Food chaser
Good gracer.

Dream thriller
Fish killer.

A: Dolphin.

Alys Davies (10)
Pen-y-Fai CiW Primary School, Bridgend

Guess Who

Swimming diver
Good driver.

She's very pretty
And has a kitty.

Good walker
Loud talker.

Very caring
And always sharing.

She's very busy
And her hair's so frizzy.

Very stunning
And very cunning.

A: My mum.

Emma Biggerstaff (10)
Pen-y-Fai CiW Primary School, Bridgend

Help! Help! Help!

'Where's the banana tree?'
Said the monkey.

Help! Help! Help!

'Where is my log?'
Said the green frog.

Help! Help! Help!

'Please don't laugh!'
Said the giraffe.

It isn't fair
Why don't you care
About us?

Lauren Sheppard (10)
Pen-y-Fai CiW Primary School, Bridgend

Doughnuts And Cake

A yummy doughnut on the table
And a yummy chocolate cake
And quickly I ate them both.

Milk and cookies

I like milk and cookies
They taste so great together
I like them for breakfast.

A cup of tea and biscuits

I like a cup of tea with biscuits
I like them together.
Yes, I have them for supper.

Samuel Gibbs (9)
Pen-y-Fai CiW Primary School, Bridgend

What Is Water

Water is a blinding wave coming from a cyclone.
It is a giant icicle lying on the land.
It is a huge snowball smashing onto Earth.
It is an ice hurricane cracking to make water.
It is a blue slush manipulating wildly.

James Picton (8)
Pen-y-Fai CiW Primary School, Bridgend

Recipe For A Bonfire

Take a colourful Catherine wheel
And a rattling Roman candle
Add a sizzling silver sparkler
Sprinkle with a rosy rampaging rocket
Cover with flaming fire.

Leah Morgan (9)
Pen-y-Fai CiW Primary School, Bridgend

Animals

Alligator

His sharp deadly teeth
Looking with gleaming eyes
Humans walk on the beach.

Snake

Poisonous fangs in his mouth
Evil reddish-black eyes
Bugs crawl unaware.

Leopard

Camouflaging himself
His spots look like pebbles
Zebra walks cluelessly.

Caitlin Price (9)
Pen-y-Fai CiW Primary School, Bridgend

Cats

Tiger lays in the grass
Waiting for his tasty prey
Zebras graze, do not know.

Cute, soft, hungry cat
Waits in the garden
Mice running clueless.

A fierce, huge lion
Hiding in the grass
Zebra drinking carelessly.

Emily Hunt (9)
Pen-y-Fai CiW Primary School, Bridgend

Christmas Comes

Christmas comes
    with children singing.

Christmas comes
    with elves making.

Christmas comes
    with snow sprinkling.

Christmas comes
    with pie-eating.

Christmas comes
    with full stockings.

Christmas comes
    with snow surfing.

Christmas comes
    with people cheering.

Christmas comes
    with snowmen smiling.

Christmas comes
    with Santa calling.

Phoebe Waters-Hussain (9)
Pen-y-Fai CiW Primary School, Bridgend

The Day Said

There came a day that caught the winter.
It caught my eye on the snow
But the snow was very low.

'What shall I do with the trees?'
The day said, the day said.
'Make the bees hibernate in the trees.'
The day said, the day said.

Juliet McKay (8)
Pen-y-Fai CiW Primary School, Bridgend

Guess Who

Catches rats
Hates bats.

Sharp jaws
Long paws.

Big jump
No bump.

Fast runner
Cod stunner.

Has lams
Like lions.

He hides
Inside.

A: Cat.

James Leppard (10)
Pen-y-Fai CiW Primary School, Bridgend

War

London 1939, Neville Chamberlain
Declared war on Germany.
The blitz wasn't enough for Hitler,
He wanted more.
World War I faded away but
Whilst this war was going on there
Weren't happy days.
Bombs, tanks, guns.

Matthew Jacka (10)
Penygawsi Primary School, Llantrisant

On The Day War Began

The sun lost its shine
Our neighbours arrived
The first gun fired
A very loud explosion
A few tanks rode by
A mother passed away
The clocks lost their tick-tocks
The children lost their sparks
The trees lost their leaves
And all ended in peace.

Joshua Jones (10)
Penygawsi Primary School, Llantrisant

War

On the day war began
The sun lost its shine
Our neighbours arrived
The trees lost their leaves
A mother lost her child
The clocks lost their chime
And a child lost her spark.

Bethan Jenkins (10)
Penygawsi Primary School, Llantrisant

Wartime

People fighting
Crashing, booming, banging
The war has ended, peace at last
Sadness.

Eloise Peacock (11)
Penygawsi Primary School, Llantrisant

War

Dead bodies,
Suffering souls,
Army tanks,
Bomb shelters,
Soldiers' crime,
Left to die,
Red, blue, black,
Got to pack,
Families cry,
Swarming jets,
Grey skies,
But comes to end,
Peace at last,
The death in the past,
Bad memories stay,
We sit to pray,
Families return,
We are home again!

Hannah Williams (11)
Penygawsi Primary School, Llantrisant

The War

The war began with killing.
Innocent people are dying.
Their loved ones are crying.
All of the politicians shouting.
The dead bodies look depressing.
But the end result is chilling.
Soldiers stop fighting.
The war ends in peace.

Naween Gamage (11)
Penygawsi Primary School, Llantrisant

War!

Planer crasher,
Machine gunner,
Brave fighter,
Terrified soldiers,
Bullet maker,
Secret sniper,
Silent killer,
Skin ripper,
Blood dripper,
First aider,
Life saver,
Hitler's fighter,
Horrible Hitler,
The hell-maker,
Jew hater,
Nasty Himmler
Hostage taker,
Concentration camper,
Death shower,
Guard tower,
Peacemaker,
Treaty paper,
American helper,
War over,
Poppy grower,
11th November
A day to remember,
Hopefully peace forever.

Ashleigh Janda (10)
Penygawsi Primary School, Llantrisant

War Colours

Black:
Black is the colour of the guns,
shooting all the time.
It is the dirt,
on the army men's faces
or black clothes,
people wear at a funeral.

Red:
Red is the colour of blood,
when innocent people have died.
It is the sunset,
when the war has eventually ended
or the red poppies lying in a field,
where dead soldiers lie.

Rosie Halford (10)
Penygawsi Primary School, Llantrisant

On The Day Battle Began

The fields lay bleeding.
The sky became shrouded in the shadow of *war*.
A soldier was dying in the pain of the battle.
The clocks were dead.
The lights went out.

On the day the battle ended

The crowds were cheering.
The sky was blue.
The towns were shouting.
The war was over.

James Clarke (10)
Penygawsi Primary School, Llantrisant

War

It's big, it's bad and they're all going mad!
Big war
Atomic war
Nuclear war
Why?
Bad war
Serious war
Civil war
Why?
World war
Bang war
Boom war
Why?
Kaboom war
Gun war
Clang war.

Ashley Evans (10)
Penygawsi Primary School, Llantrisant

Atomic War Kennings

Plane flyer
Bomb dropper
Gun shooter
People killer
Heart snatcher
Body rotter
Fun robber.

Why!

Amber Evans (10)
Penygawsi Primary School, Llantrisant

War

On the day war began:
The sun stopped shining
The trees stopped swaying
The plants stopped blooming
A mother started crying
And the clocks stopped ticking
The lights were dull.

On the day war ended:
The clouds moved again
The crowds were building
Old soldiers were dead but they died for us
A bugle sounded
The children played.

Scott Thomas (11)
Penygawsi Primary School, Llantrisant

War - Haikus

Wars are terrible,
Lots of helpless people die.
War is over, peace.

Wars keep on coming,
They will never, ever end.
People keep dying.

Matthew Freeman (11)
Penygawsi Primary School, Llantrisant

At The Seaside

In the rock pools,
Creatures swim around,
Some in the water,
Some on the ground.

Salty air covers the beach,
The colour of the sand,
Is sort of peach.

Fish in the water,
Shells on the sand,
Starfish are floating,
And a crab pinched my hand!

When I'm at the beach,
I always have fun,
And when I'm feeling hungry,
I have a sausage in a bun.

Boats are sailing slowly on the sea,
The wind is blowing,
Slowly around me.

Natasha Vincent (8)
Penygawsi Primary School, Llantrisant

War - Haikus

Wars are horrible,
Some innocent people die,
Every war must stop.

But wars keep coming,
Soldiers fight for their country,
Blood keeps getting spilt.

At last peace has come,
Presidents feast together,
And everyone cheers.

Cyrus Kehl (11)
Penygawsi Primary School, Llantrisant

War

Children hiding in shelters,
Bombs falling from the sky,
Army tanks ride into fight,
Guns shooting at innocent families,
All you can hear is cries and screams,
Blood running down the streets of London,
It's grey, horrible and gloomy in the misty clouds.
The war ended,
The sun came out,
The sky turned blue,
People came out of shelters,
Everybody reunited with their families and loved ones.
Peace at last.

Amy Griffiths (11)
Penygawsi Primary School, Llantrisant

War Kennings

Gun firer,
Cannonball shooter,
Brave soldier,
Plane crasher,
Person killer,
Bad Hitler,
Plane flyer,
Terrified soldier.

Dylan Legg (9)
Penygawsi Primary School, Llantrisant

War

Boom! All the guns go bang!
Killing everyone till their heads go clang.
When the sergeant says, 'Hold!'
And we already go.
Once they give up, then we know that we've won.

Once we have won, we get really famous,
Just so the president doesn't really blame us,
When they raise their flag,
We put them in a bag,
Look at them now, struggling to kill us.

'Let's celebrate!' we altogether said.
Just before we went to bed,
We all thought how we combined
We also had a glass of wine.
'I'm going to bed,' whimpered Ed.
Yeah!

Joshua McFarlane (11)
Penygawsi Primary School, Llantrisant

December

D ecember is coming, the snow is near,
E ating Christmas dinner,
C hrist Jesus' birthday today!
E verything is decorated,
M eeting your relatives,
B elieving in jolly Santa Claus,
E xciting gifts to buy,
R emembering to write Christmas cards!

Mia Fogerty (8)
Penygawsi Primary School, Llantrisant

War

Bloody bodies
Giant tanks
Loud guns
Red blood
Demolished houses
Hard shelters
Peace at last
Mess is cleaned
Loved ones back
Happy faces
Families reunited
Sad faces.

Lucy Giles (11)
Penygawsi Primary School, Llantrisant

War Is Here!

W orry is all around us
A ll that can be heard is bangs
R iots are approaching us fast

I mprisonment suffocates us all
S creams can be heard everywhere

H atred is all we feel
E vacuation is happening all the time
R ed blood is running like a stream
E xplosions that put fear on all children.

Lucy Ross (11)
Penygawsi Primary School, Llantrisant

I Wish I'd Looked After My Teeth!

(Inspired by 'Oh, I Wish I'd Looked After Me Teeth' by Pam Ayres)

One day I went to the dentist,
I hoped my teeth were the bestest.

I wanted clean small ones,
I wanted clean tall ones,
Not a speck of decay in sight.

The dentist said to my mother,
'Does she brush her teeth?'

'Well . . . she did not brush them this morning,
She did not brush them the past eight nights,
She did not brush them last year,
She did not brush them last night.'

Oh! I wish I'd looked after my teeth,
I wish they were sparkling white with relief.

Oh! I wish I'd looked after my teeth,
I ran home to cry in my handkerchief!

Chloe Rees (8)
Penygawsi Primary School, Llantrisant

March

M erry March
A rrived so soon,
R emember to wish
C hloe Freeman
H appy birthday!

Chloe Freeman (8)
Penygawsi Primary School, Llantrisant

A Recipe For A Cat

(Based on 'Recipe For A Hippopotamus Sandwich' by Shel Silverstein)

A cat sandwich is easy to make,
All you do is simply take,
One slice of bread,
One slice of fish,
Some mayonnaise,
One onion ring,
One cat,
One piece of string,
A sprinkle of pepper,
That ought to do it.
And now comes the problem,
Biting into it.

Lauren Paskell (8)
Penygawsi Primary School, Llantrisant

The War Will Never End

A dramatic war will never end
Fighting will never stop
Run before they get you, you never want to be there
As fast as a bullet
I do hope they will go some time this week
Do listen to this message, so be brave, don't be afraid.

Abigail Kidley (11)
Plasyfelin Primary School, Caerphilly

The Chimney

I loved it when the fire started
And I would bellow out my smoke
I loved it in the winter
When they gave the fire a poke
But because of central heating
I sit and look at the sky
I talk to my friends, the aerials
And often wonder why
Please do not ignore me
I always try to smile
Because as things develop
I won't be here in a while.

Bethan Harris (10)
Plasyfelin Primary School, Caerphilly

Old People

O ld people sometimes like to go out,
L ying in the sun or getting about,
D own in the cellar is where they get the doubt.

P eople who are old sometimes like to have visitors,
E ven if it is their own family,
O ver the road lives their elderly friend,
P eople like to show things to them,
L etting them come into their house,
E lderly people can sometimes be good.

Cassandra Jones (10)
Plasyfelin Primary School, Caerphilly

Old People

Why are old people so slow?
Is it because their hearts are so old?
Old people never go with the flow
Most are no longer bold, but some are.
Why are they no longer allowed in bars?
Why do most old people wear glasses?
Why do old people get scars?
We don't think it's fair.
People are always shouting at them in a harsh way,
So there they lie in so much pain.
It almost seems they look so frail, slow, old . . .

Molly Jayne Kinrade (10)
Plasyfelin Primary School, Caerphilly

Egyptian Poetry

The pyramids are for one person
The Egyptians built the biggest pyramids
For all the treasures
Golden lions, tigers and cats
Standing in a row
Waiting for the pharaoh to come,
The treasure is safe.

Lucie John (8)
Plasyfelin Primary School, Caerphilly

Old People

(A true story)

Why are old people sometimes nasty?
Is it because they are afraid?
Isn't it nice to have grandparents to look after you,
get you stuff you don't need?
I was very lucky because my nan
stayed alive for eight years.
But when I was eight and a half
and my mum was giving birth to my sister,
Nan and I saw her.
The next day my nan went into hospital for a week,
Then she died.
That's why I have feelings for old people.

Luke Formosa (10)
Plasyfelin Primary School, Caerphilly

Old People

Old people are very kind to me.
Old people are quite slow like me.
Old people can be lazy just like me.
Old people are patient like me.
Old people make me feel happy.
Old people look sad.
Old people like seeing me and my dad.

David Joseph White (10)
Plasyfelin Primary School, Caerphilly

Old People

I like old people
They are so friendly
They give you treats
And loads of sweets
Old people have feelings
For family and friends
They really do care
And they love a big, huge teddy bear
I really look out for them
They also look out for me
They always give me lemonade
And they take me to the arcade.

Sarah-Louise Cartwright (10)
Plasyfelin Primary School, Caerphilly

Blue

Blue is the colour of the sea
rushing up and down.
Blue is the sky
staying still and almost always quiet.
Blue is a carpet,
smooth and soft.
Blue is like a book
filled with words.
Big blue eyes,
scanning a room.
Nice blue socks comforting your feet.

James Lewis (9)
Plasyfelin Primary School, Caerphilly

The Learning Of Sirius

I believe in the dog star Sirius
Thinking about it makes me feel delirious

It's a constellation in the heavens above
A star of dignity, leadership and love

Is this the place where dogs come to die
Or is it just a big rock in the sky?

The dog star shines bright, letting cats prowl
But would the Earth shake if it were to growl?

I have also wondered what type of breed
A big dog like a German Shepherd, yes indeed

I am mad about dogs
A little too mad, I think

Did you enjoy the subject on Sirius
Or instead, did it make you feel hilarious?

Jennifer Siemes (10)
Plasyfelin Primary School, Caerphilly

Mother, Mother

Mother, Mother, you're the worst
When you have that temper burst.

Mother, Mother, you're so great
I wish you were my mate

Mother, Mother, you're so kind
I really love you all the time.

Liam Evans (9)
Plasyfelin Primary School, Caerphilly

Dancing

I've wanted to dance since I could walk
Or was it before I could talk?
I've watched the dancing on TV
And thought, *one day that could be me.*
I started to dance at the age of four
And ever since have danced more and more
I dance at weekends three times, sometimes four
But never do I find it a bore
I have a dance partner called Elena
She is only six days older than me
We practise together all the time
Either at her house, or at mine
Every couple of months we have a dance test
My partner and I do our best
Sometimes we lose
Sometimes we win
But at the end of the day, we know we've been.

Carlie Billingham (9)
Plasyfelin Primary School, Caerphilly

The Weather

One morning I stepped out of my door
and the weather was freezing, teasing but pleasing.

The next morning the weather was appalling,
there was so much rain it was a pain.

That evening I looked out of my window,
there was thunder and lightning,
it was oh, so frightening!

So now you've learnt that the weather is clever,
never ever underestimate the weather!

Lewys Grother (8)
Plasyfelin Primary School, Caerphilly

Red

Red is the colour of Liverpool
the team that I support.
Red is the colour of a car
convertible, lush as can be.
Red is the colour of leaves
falling from the trees.
Red is the colour of a pen
for teachers or you and me.
Red is the colour of sunburn
that's on your arm.
Red is the colour of a fox
sneaking in the night.
Red is the colour of shoes
sandals, high heels or boots.
Red is the colour of the dragon
standing on the Welsh flag.

Leah Marie Richards (10)
Plasyfelin Primary School, Caerphilly

Tropical Storm

The sky is getting darker.
Clouds are moving fast.
Wind is blowing stronger.
Palm trees are bending, touching the ground.
Debris is flung through the air.
Huge waves are crashing into the shore.
Lightning illuminates the island.
Thunder is heard for miles around.

Conor Atwood (9)
Plasyfelin Primary School, Caerphilly

The Jungle

Deep in the jungle
Live tigers, snakes and bugs
Leopards and monkeys
Even some slugs.
They creep and they crawl
They roar and they maul
From the tiniest ant
To the lion - king of them all.
From treetop to ground
Nature's beasts all around.
Thank goodness I live
In a nice, quiet town.

Ieuan Easterbrook (8)
Plasyfelin Primary School, Caerphilly

A Rainbow

Red is the colour of a berry
Orange is the colour of a tiger
Yellow is the colour of the sun
Green is the colour of the grass
Blue is the colour of the sky
Indigo is the colour of a drop of ink
Violet is the colour of a bluebell
The rainbow makes us smile
Every time we look to the sky.

Carys Grother (10)
Plasyfelin Primary School, Caerphilly

The Seed Factory

First the factory bursts open,
And wires spill out loud.
Then the poles tower up,
Way above the ground.
Suddenly huge car parks form,
Big, green and round.
Then colourful helicopter pads
Form without a sound.

Then the big buzzy bees,
Land and take the money.
They take it back to their hive,
And turn it into honey.
Then the fruits start to grow,
And are picked for mango chutney.
This is thanks to the tiny seed
That helped build our country.

Liam Atwood (11)
Plasyfelin Primary School, Caerphilly

Old People

Old people have feelings
just like me and you
of old people from the past
like every old shoe

They're loving and caring
about everything
especially when it comes to family
they can't resist a thing.

Naomi Griffiths (10)
Plasyfelin Primary School, Caerphilly

My Dog Molly

I love my dog Molly
She loves me too
I give her cuddles
And she gets my shoes.
I walk to the door
She gets there first
I put her lead on
And away she goes.
She heads for the park
Where I throw the ball
But she chases the ducks
And we can't find the ball.
It gets very dark and I'm very cold
So I call, *'Molly!*
We're going home!'

Benedict Kilburn (9)
Plasyfelin Primary School, Caerphilly

Let's Go Fishing

If you have a rod
and some wire,
a couple of hooks
and a float.
Don't forget bait
and food for you.
You're all set
and off you go.

Iwan John Gane (9)
Plasyfelin Primary School, Caerphilly

My Puppy Dog

Molly is my puppy dog,
Molly is my friend,
Molly dog will stay with me
Devoted to the end.

She's coloured black with four white socks,
Her belly is white too,
She's playful and she's loving
And cheeky through and through.

She likes to mess my room up
When I'm sleeping in my bed,
And then she jumps on top of me
And licks all of my head!

When she's in the living room
She drives my daddy wild,
By jumping up onto his lap
And acting like a child.

When she has been naughty
She lies flat on the ground,
Her head upon her two front paws,
Her sad eyes looking round.

Molly loves the water,
She's learning how to swim,
I hope that all the exercise
Will keep her nice and slim.

Now it's dark, she's fast asleep,
It isn't what it seems,
As I lie sleeping in my bed
She's playing in my dreams!

Emily Jayne Jones (9)
Plasyfelin Primary School, Caerphilly

Green

Grass
which is really
fresh in summer.

Apples
they are really
sweet and delicious.

Peas
they can roll around
In every direction.

Grape
a sort of ball
that is the best
fruit of all.

Leaves
that turn a lush colour
in autumn.

A car
that we can travel
around the world in.

Cabbage
I have it with
a Sunday dinner.

Caerphilly
my team I play for
in rugby.

Liam Taviner (10)
Plasyfelin Primary School, Caerphilly

Stroppy Poppy

I have a cat, her name is Poppy,
Sometimes happy, but mostly stroppy.
She sleeps all day and runs round at night,
Waking my mum. What a sight!

She eats a lot and has a big belly
And sits with me sometimes and watches the telly.
She has gorgeous black fur and huge green eyes
And when ready to hunt, looks up to the skies.

She chases the birds and rats and mice
Which really isn't very nice.
Always miaowing and causing a scene,
She's the stroppiest cat there has ever been.

I cuddle her when she's in a good mood,
But it's usually only because she wants food.
When she hisses she can really scare you,
Try and stroke her then - I dare you!

With great big claws and giant paws,
She's really good at opening doors.
She tries to escape when locked in a room.
Open the door and off she goes - *zoom!*

So that's the story of Stroppy Poppy,
Great big cat who underneath it all, is soppy.
She sneaks a cuddle when no one's around.
Then purring is the only sound!

Tamara Blackler (9)
Plasyfelin Primary School, Caerphilly

Splish, Splash, Splosh

Splish, splash, splosh
Water, it's everywhere
Water, it's in my hair
But I don't care.

Splish, splash, splosh
Water, it's everywhere
It keeps us healthy,
We bathe, we shower in it
Sometimes people drink it.

Splish, splash, splosh
Water, it's everywhere
Water, it's animals' homes
Dolphins, whales, fish
Big ones, small ones
And any sizes.

Splish, splash, splosh
Water, it's everywhere
Water, all different colours
Blue, sparkling
Crystal clear
Everyone remember
Water will always be near.

Splish, splash, splosh
Splish, splash, splosh
Water is everywhere
Splish, splash, splosh.

Abbie Waters (11)
Plasyfelin Primary School, Caerphilly

Pets

I love pets in every way,
They love to play every day,
They make different noises and different sounds,
Like a pack of hunting hounds!
They dance and dance,
And they prance and prance,
They can be a rabbit, they can be a cat, they can be a dog,
Though I doubt it's a frog!
They can be happy, they can be sad,
They can be angry or they can be mad!

Kayleigh Ashman (9)
Plasyfelin Primary School, Caerphilly

The Tropical Island

Birds are singing softly.
I can hear the sea sing quietly to me.
The sand is alive, it's brushing slowly in the deep blue sea.
The sun is bright like there's a dragon in sight.
Then I see juicy fruit hanging from a palm tree.
I can hear the air; it's rushing past really fast.
The waves are as calm and shiny as can be,
Just count, one, two, three.

Chakayler Jeffery (10)
Plasyfelin Primary School, Caerphilly

Dispersal

D ancing seeds
I n the wind they move,
S eeking their next location.
P op onto the ground.
E xcretion by animals,
R ivers as well.
S eeds that are small or big,
A re all dispersed in some way,
L ight and fluffy their texture is!

Leona Vaughan (11)
Plasyfelin Primary School, Caerphilly

My Little Sister

My little sister, her name is Grace,
She is small and cute with a pretty face.
We get in a fight and I have to yell,
My mother says, 'Do I need a bell?'
She kicks the dog and squeezes the cat
And has a tantrum on her mat.
She jumps up and down and is never still,
But I love her and I always will.

Molly Oldham (9)
Plasyfelin Primary School, Caerphilly

My Garden

In my nanny's garden
we have a flower patch.
We've dug it and weeded it
and made it all from scratch.
We've planted lots of flowers
and special veggies too.
We're waiting now for them to grow
so we can have
some
stew!

Keiran Hughes (8)
Plasyfelin Primary School, Caerphilly

Animals' Coats

All animals have coats,
Furry, soft, smooth and wet.
A furry goat has a woolly jacket,
A slithering snake has a scaly skin,
A colourful bird has colourful feathers,
A wet whale has wet skin that swishes the waves.
What a different place to live.

Iain Barnett (11)
Plasyfelin Primary School, Caerphilly

Hooray For Summer

The winter has passed, the rain is over
The flowers appear through the earth
The time of singing birds is here
Summer is on its way, I can't wait
To go out to play, hip hip hooray!

Mark Lee Morgan (9)
Plasyfelin Primary School, Caerphilly

The Quarrel

I quarrelled with my brother,
I don't know what about,
One thing led to another,
And somehow we fell out.
The start of it was slight,
The end of it was strong,
He said he was right,
I knew he was wrong!

We hated one another.
The afternoon turned black!

Hannah Williams (8)
Plasyfelin Primary School, Caerphilly

Water, Water

Water, water everywhere.
Water, water in my hair.
Water, water in the pipes.
Water, water in the sink.
Water, water falls from the sky.
Water, water on the floor.
Water, water, you can have fun.
Water, water can break your bones.
Water, water can wash your clothes.

Rebecca A Morkot (8)
Plasyfelin Primary School, Caerphilly

Thunder And Lightning

Thunder and lightning, loud and bright
Dark docks, sailing boats, flashing light
Rain scattering across Caerphilly
Barking dogs running by the Piccadilly
Deep fog, hard to see
No sight of me!

Reuben Roberts-Garcia (9)
Plasyfelin Primary School, Caerphilly

s

is very tall
and very strong.
But this is not all
and I am not wrong.
She gets excited when I shout 'Walk!'
She barks at me, but cannot talk.
She finds her bone by the garden wall,
she brings it back to show us all.

This is my dog, Jess.
But oh, what a mess!
She finds the mud and rolls about,
then you'll hear my mum shout!

But she's my dog, Jess,
and I love her the best
even though she is a pest.

Daniel Thomas (9)
Plasyfelin Primary School, Caerphilly

Old People

O ld people are sometimes fun,
L ike the morning rising sun,
D own the house with hot cross buns.

P eople always say
E lderly people sleep in the day.
O n the hour in the chair,
P eople just must take care.
L ovely people, can't you see
E lderly people are like you and me?

Hannah Walby (10)
Plasyfelin Primary School, Caerphilly

Electricity

One million shocking volts
Flowing through the circuit
The sun comes out at midnight
When lightning's prowling the night
A power cut all through the land
TVs off, computers frozen
Everywhere goes blank
Metal conductors
Plastic insulators
Rubber makes you safe
Electricity runs our world
But it can also end it.

Dylan Morgan (11)
Plasyfelin Primary School, Caerphilly

Water

Water, water everywhere,
teensy-weensy pearls sparkle in the moonlight.
Water drops hit the ground
and form a puddle of diamond drops.

Water, water everywhere,
too many drops to count.
You swim, you bathe, you drink it,
and that's how much it counts!

Ashleigh Jane Farrow (11)
Plasyfelin Primary School, Caerphilly

Rivers And Seas

I hear the roaring waves,
Crashing against the rocks,
Clear, crystal-blue.
Rough ripples, flowing downstream,
Full of wonder, full of clues.

The turquoise sea,
With streaks of green.
Sometimes happy,
Sometimes mean.

The sort of sea,
That I'm talking about.
The two-faced creature
Has no doubt.

Keira Saunders (11)
Plasyfelin Primary School, Caerphilly

What Can You Do?

What can you do?
I can swim.
What can you do?
I can horseride.
What can you do?
I can skate.
What can you do?
I can ride a bike.
What can you do?
I can do anything
If I really try.

Emma Nicole Vaughan (9)
Plasyfelin Primary School, Caerphilly

Pyramid Treasures

When you go down
to the pyramid,
prepare to be amazed,
gold, gold and gold
waiting to be taken away.
Careful, you don't wake the pharaoh
waiting in his tomb . . .
'Why don't you back off
or I will get you too!'

Kirsty Douglas (8)
Plasyfelin Primary School, Caerphilly

On A Starry Night

On a starry night
When the moon was bright
Earth lay sleeping
Not a sound could be heard
Stars twinkling in the night sky
Beautifully spread across the sky
Sparkling like diamonds on a velvet cloth
Peering over Earth like a guardian angel.

I love starry nights!

Ashley Evans (9)
Plasyfelin Primary School, Caerphilly

Organs

The human organs help us live,
They help us breathe, move and give,
A time for fun and play and being active,
I have two lungs and kidneys two,
One heart and a liver that make me function through.

Jonathan Davies (11)
Plasyfelin Primary School, Caerphilly

My Dog Ellie

I have a Jack Russell, her name is Ellie May,
She's cute and funny and has fun every day.
Ellie can play football, she can stop me scoring goals
And when we watch DIY SOS, she barks at Mr Knowles!
We taught her how to use the dog flap,
She now uses it with ease,
She wears a pink collar to stop her having fleas.
We bought her a juicy bone,
She munched it long and hard,
She did a whoopsie which Dad didn't see
And he slipped out in the yard!

Harry Paterson (9)
Plasyfelin Primary School, Caerphilly

Egyptian Treasure

Twinkling treasures, sparkling bright
Most of it is gold
Glistening in the light
The pharaohs are in their golden case
Each of them has a golden face
Colourful paintings on the walls
Blue, red, green and yellow
Statues stand guard over the golden treasure
Like the Egyptians frozen in time.

Leigh-Ann Hewer (8)
Plasyfelin Primary School, Caerphilly

Habitats

Fish swim around in the lake,
Rabbits bounce around the meadow,
Worms slide under the soil,
Bats fly around the cave,
Birds sing in the trees,
Camels trot in the forest.

All different habitats,
For all different species.

Andrew Morgan (11)
Plasyfelin Primary School, Caerphilly

Senses

S ee with my eyes
E ars to hear
N ose to smell
S ort with my hands
E yes to look at the world
S ensation in my mouth.

Ryan Kinrade (11)
Plasyfelin Primary School, Caerphilly

A Tiger's Day!

The mother tiger protects her cubs.
The father gets the food,
He pounces and runs
To catch his prey.

That's a tiger's day!

Amber Williams (11)
Plasyfelin Primary School, Caerphilly

Water, Water!

Water, water everywhere
Water, water in the puddles there
Water, water in the sky
My mum said it's when God cries!

Water, water everywhere
In the shower
In my hair
That's why people stare!

Water, water everywhere
And not a drop to drink
Water, water everywhere
What a terrible *stink!*

Green and blue
Is the colour of the sea
Sparkling and clear
Is the colour of the stream!

Water in my shower
Water in my bath
Water in my sink
Tickles my feet and makes me laugh!

Ha, ha, ha!

Shinae Williams (11)
Plasyfelin Primary School, Caerphilly

Old People

Old people are different to me
Old people don't like me
Old people have wrinkly skin
Old people don't like me
Because I climb on their trees.

Cejay Leitis (9)
Plasyfelin Primary School, Caerphilly

My Friend

I have a friend
She's a special friend
On her I can depend

When I feel sad
She makes me feel glad
She sometimes makes me very mad!

Together we listen and share
About each other, we will always care!

She has a beauty
She has a trend
She'll be my friend
Until the end.

Emma Hobbs (9)
Plasyfelin Primary School, Caerphilly

Beautiful Dragonflies

Dragonflies dancing in the air,
Twisting and twirling everywhere.
Showing off their colourful wings,
Just like rainbows, such beautiful things!

Asha Davies (8)
Plasyfelin Primary School, Caerphilly

The Nile

The Nile is a big river flowing through Egypt.
In September the Nile floods,
In the summer the Nile goes back,
Then people can grow their vegetables.

Emily Smith (7)
Plasyfelin Primary School, Caerphilly

Old People

Old people are funny to me,
They tell stupid jokes.
They think old songs are better than the new ones.
They dress in light colours.
They wear knobbly shoes.
They often have scruffy old cats.
They try to make me eat veg
And they have stupid 'welcome' mats.
They take out their teeth and put them in a glass of water.
They wear wigs and clip-on earrings.
They are your friends,
But that is sometimes hard to see.

Charlotte Emerson
Plasyfelin Primary School, Caerphilly

Old People

I like old people, they spoil you.
They give you sweets and take you to the park.
I like old people, they tell you stories.
They tell you stories of when they were young and about the war.
But best of all are your grandparents,
They hug you with their warm jumpers on
And tell you they love you very much.

Curtis John Perrett (10)
Plasyfelin Primary School, Caerphilly

Wild Animals

Deep in the jungle animals play in a wild sort of way.
They really enjoy it, I hope they don't mind
If I tell a lie that one of them went to hide.
I searched on and on until I saw a distant thing,
I was so surprised but it was nothing.
I dreamt I was in the jungle, yes it was all a dream
Quite sad, but I was happy,
Still, I really wish that it was real.
'But wait! What's that noise up ahead?'
I think it's a volcano
(Oh never mind),
It's behind me anyway.
I'll keep that dream for another night.

Matthew Day (7)
Plasyfelin Primary School, Caerphilly

My Dog Amber

My dog is so nice, she doesn't even bite.
My dog never chews the mail.
My dog is always pleased to see us.
My dog sometimes barks at the visitors.
My dog sometimes barks at the birds.
She's always pleased to play with me.
My dog, my dog, my dog!

Sean Davies (7)
Plasyfelin Primary School, Caerphilly

Summer

Summer is fun
Summer is fun
Fun, fun, fun, fun, fun
You can run in the summer
Run in the summer
Run, run, run, run, run
You can play in the summer
Play in the summer
Play, play, play, play, play
You can swim in the summer
Swim in the summer
Swim, swim, swim, swim, swim.

Rhiannon Watkins (7)
Plasyfelin Primary School, Caerphilly

My Dreams

I dreamt I could fly up in the sky.
I dreamt that I could swim like a fish.
I dreamt, I dreamt and I dreamt.
I dreamt about my birthday and Christmas,
All the presents and cards.
I dreamt that I had lots of friends,
And more cousins and family,
And even mums and dads.
I dreamt . . .

Chloe Evans (7)
Plasyfelin Primary School, Caerphilly

My Dog

My dog likes meat
She also steals my seat
She sucks on a bone
When she's all alone
After that I put her food down
She plays like she's a clown
Wearing her big, hairy frown.

Ryan J Williams (7)
Plasyfelin Primary School, Caerphilly

What Is Blue?

Blue is the colour,
When you're happy or sad,
Blue is the colour when you're feeling bad,
Blue is the colour of the flowers in the park,
Blue is the colour of a flying lark.

Blue is the colour of an evening sky,
Blue is the colour of a blueberry pie,
Blue is the colour of a school cardigan,
Blue is the colour of my teacher's staple gun,

Blue is the colour,
And not the only one,
Blue is the colour of us having fun!

Charlotte Bevan (11)
St James' Primary School, Caerphilly

What Is Blue?

Blue is the colour of the sky.
Blue is the colour of the sea.
Blue is the colour of Chelsea FC.
Blue is the colour of Neptune, the planet.
Blue is the colour of Uranus, the planet.
Blue is sad to a human eye.
Blue is cold to a human eye.
Blue is the colour of something cold.
Blue is the colour of disgusting mould.
Blue is the colour of some kind of cloth.
Blue is the colour of a moth.
Blue is the colour of the whooshing wind.
Blue is the best colour known to Man.

Joe Hughes (11)
St James' Primary School, Caerphilly

What Is Red?

Red is the colour of anger and rage,
the colour of a red, red rose.
Red is a bloodshot nose,
a blazing phoenix in the air.
Red is the colour of exploding fireworks in the sky,
also the colour of the Devil's eyes.
Red is the colour of dripping blood,
red as a ruby, a lot of money.
Red is the colour of a Jammy Dodger.
Red is the colour of a flaming ring.
So that's what red is!

Andrew Hill (11)
St James' Primary School, Caerphilly

What Is Yellow?

Yellow is the sun that shines on me.
The sound I like to hear on a summer's day.
Yellow is where people laugh and play.
I like the daffodils because of the smell.
It's even a flower that girls like to wear,
A lion, a tiger, and even the giraffe.
There might even be a yellow brick road.
Yellow is a band I like to wear
I touch a yellow pineapple skin.
Yellow is gold's baby.
Yellow is a star in the scary sky.

Laura Dyer (10)
St James' Primary School, Caerphilly

What Is Red?

Red is the colour of the blazing sun.
Red is the colour of a ruby ring,
Also the colour of a flaming phoenix.
Red is the colour of the planet Mars,
Also the twinkle in the Devil's eyes.
Red is the colour of Jupiter's spot,
Where a raging storm has never stopped.
Red is the blood when you cut your hand.
Red is the colour of anger and rage.
This is red.

Daniel Case (10)
St James' Primary School, Caerphilly

What Is Red?

Red is the colour of love in your heart,
but it can hurt when it breaks apart.
Red is the colour of scales on a fish,
glistening and sparkling and changing so quick.
Red is the colour of danger inside,
and it can bring you mad red eyes.
Red is the sunset at the start of night.
Red is the fire spitting out light.
Red are the roses, as sweet as can be.
Red is the most splendid colour to see.

Red is the sunburn burning your skin.
Red is a lobster, tasty and thin.
Red is the sunshine burning away.
Red are the leaves on an autumn's day.
Red is a ruby, sparkly and sweet.
Red is the busiest colour to be.

Danielle Connor (11)
St James' Primary School, Caerphilly

What Is Gold?

It's a gold, sparkling star shooting across the midnight sky.
Gold is a smooth soft piece of silk.
Gold is the soft touch of a fully grown daffodil.
Gold is a nugget, as tasty as can be.
Gold is like lightning streaking through the darkest sky.
It's gold, it's gold, the magnificent colour for me.
Gold, gold is joyful and happy.
Whenever I see gold, it makes me feel rich.

Jake Fletcher (11)
St James' Primary School, Caerphilly

What Is Gold?

Gold is a trophy when you win at football
Gold is a star that's in the sky
Gold is the blazing sun that shines
Gold is a teddy that's in the market
Gold is number 1!

Gold is a hamster running around
Gold is a pound coin you spend on sweets
Gold is the sand of Porthcawl beach.

When I stick my hand in gold paint
Gold is the colour of my hand.
Gold is a metal that is grand.

Shannon Livingstone (10)
St James' Primary School, Caerphilly

What Is Blue?

Blue is the colour of the sky,
Blue is the wind passing by.

Blue is the colour of Neptune up there,
Blue is the colour of an eye of a bear.

Blue is when you're sad and cold,
Blue is the colour of disgusting mould.

Blue is a bluebell on the ground,
Blue is an icicle sound.

Blue is the colour of the sea,
Blue is the best colour to be.

Ryan Thomas (11)
St James' Primary School, Caerphilly

Friends

My name is Jiggly Jordan
And my friend's name is Jumping Johnny,
We come from Junior Jamaica
And we love juicy juice.

My name is Sly Sophie
And my friend's name is Silly Sue,
We come from sunny Sweden
And we love smelly socks.

My name is Bouncing Benny
And my friend's name is Big Betty,
We come from Bonny Barnsley
And we like barking benches.

My name is Annoying Angharad
And my friend's name is Alarming Arnold,
We come from angry Ashford
And we love any apricots.

Jordan Carter (9)
St James' Primary School, Caerphilly

What Is Red?

Red is the colour of a ruby ring.
Red is like a fire burning bright.
Red is like a volcano exploding with lava.
Red is the feeling when you are angry.
Fed is the colour of a fire-breathing phoenix.
Red is the slimy blood when you cut your hand.
Red is the colour of sunburn.
Red is the colour of a blazing sun.

Steffan Rees (10)
St James' Primary School, Caerphilly

What Is Lilac?

Lilac's the colour of a soft duvet.
Sometimes it blends when it's sunset.
It smells of tulips, yes, that's the colour.
Cold sweets make you think of lilac.
My mum and dad have lilac stone rings.

Colours are my favourite things.
Lilac you can get for football team tops.
It's cool weather in the sky above
And sometimes a collar on a dove.
You can be pretty in every condition.
Really better than a top musician.

Rhea Smith (10)
St James' Primary School, Caerphilly

Friends

My name is Cute Chloe
And my friend is Charming Charlie.
We come from cool Cardiff
And we like chilly clubs.

My friend's name is Smiley Siân
And we come from sunny Swansea.
We like strawberry soap.

My friend's name is Tomato Tess
And her friend is Telling Tom,
And we come from Toddler Town.

Chloe Brindle (8)
St James' Primary School, Caerphilly

Friends

My name is Behave Bethan
And my friend is Bossy Betty
We come from beautiful Birmingham
And we like birthdays

My name is Calm Chloe
And my friend is Chatty Cathy
We come from cold Caerphilly
And we like cookies

My name is Dancing Daniel
And my friend is Daft Darren
We come from daring Devon
And we like dandelions

My name is Eating Ellie
And my friend is Easy Emma
We come from even Europe
And we like eggs

My name is Fussy Fiona
And my friend is Fancy Fion
We come from famous France
And we like flowers

My name is Gentle Genna
And my friend is Generous George
We come from genius Germany
And we like gems

My name is Helpful Henry
And my friend is Heavy Harry
We come from hot Humberside
And we like honey.

Bethan Williams (9)
St James' Primary School, Caerphilly

Awesome Alliteration!

My name is Beautiful Bethan
And my friend is Barging Bella
We come from big Birmingham
And we love bouncing balls.

My name is New Nicola
And my friend is Naughty Nicole
We come from neat New York
And we love nervous netball!

My name is Yawning Yasmin
And my friend is Young Yvonne
We come from yappy Yorkshire
And we like yummy Yorkshire pudding!

Bethan Davies (8)
St James' Primary School, Caerphilly

Awesome Alliteration!

My name is Jumping Jemma
And my friend is Jagged Jade
We come from jolly Jamaica
And we love jolly juggling!

My name is Kicking Kailum
And my friend is Kind Katie
We come from kicking Kent
And we love kick-boxing!

My name is Loopy Lauren
And my friend is Looking Lori
We come from loopy Lincolnshire
And we like licking luscious lollies!

Jemma Cook (8)
St James' Primary School, Caerphilly

What Is Yellow?

Buttercups are yellow, swaying in the breeze,
Daffodils are dancing, leaning side to side.
Bananas and lemons are yellow but taste totally different.

A spark of yellow lightning,
A clear, sunny day,
A bumblebee, a leopard and a budgie,
Lions, cheetahs and parrots are yellow.

Keys that glisten in the sun,
Stars that are twinkling in the dark sky,
Yellow reminds me of all these!

Natasha Seaward (11)
St James' Primary School, Caerphilly

What Is Red?

Red is to fire as the sun is to Earth
The red ant runs like a mouse across the ground
Red is like an exploding volcano with lava shooting out
Red is a fire engine accelerating through the street
Red is a cut on your hand when blood comes out
Red is, of course, the beautiful sunset
When you are angry you are seeing red.

Kristian Davies (10)
St James' Primary School, Caerphilly

What Is Green?

Green is the colour of slime,
Green is the sweet smell of the grass,
Green is an amazing colour,
Green is a snake,
Green is the view of the countryside,
Green is a turtle,
Green is a feeling of sick.

Cory Wills (11)
St James' Primary School, Caerphilly

A Wizard

A wizard has faith,
A wizard has power,
He has a great mind
And lives in a tower.

The wizard has a unicorn,
The most magical animal in the world,
A unicorn horn has magic dust,
It's pretty and it's curled.

A wizard has a long life,
More than one hundred years, in fact,
Trolls and witches are the same,
And they live in his big sack!

Rebecca Boyce (11)
Ysgol Gymraeg Bro Ogwr, Bridgend

My Family

I have a stepbrother called Owen who's silly
Like the cartoon character, Billy.
I have a brother called Josh who's cool
Instead of a fool.
I have a stepdad called Steve, who's strong
Like Kong.
I have a dad called Marcus, who's into sport
Instead of the news about a court.
I have a mum called Leanne who's pretty
Like the kitty.
I'm Rhys who likes school
Like a pool.

Rhys Hughes (9)
Ysgol Gymraeg Bro Ogwr, Bridgend

My Dog Scruffy

Scruffy is our dog
he tries to be good
but is always bad!
He is naughty and runs away
even when we tell him . . .
'Stay!'

We look for him everywhere
but he doesn't care.
Sometimes he comes home late
perhaps he has been on a date!

We love him even though he's bad.
When he's told off he looks so sad.
But he doesn't listen at all,
come on Scruffy, get your ball.

Daniel Higgins (10)
Ysgol Gymraeg Bro Ogwr, Bridgend

The Silly Man

There once was a man called Bill,
He really wanted a pill,
He touched some mice,
He thought that was nice,
And then he bumped his head on the bed,
And then he got fed,
And soon he was dead.

Levi Pollard (11)
Ysgol Gymraeg Bro Ogwr, Bridgend

Animals

Animals can be fuzzy, furry or fluffy,
Some are well-groomed and some can be scruffy.

Some have long necks and are very tall,
Others are short, stumpy and small.

Some can swim and some can fly,
Animals lived before you and I.

Some can roar and some can bleat,
Some eat veg and some eat meat!

Scales, fur, paws and wings
Animals . . . we're funny things!

Abbie Walker (10)
Ysgol Gymraeg Bro Ogwr, Bridgend

The Two Young Boys

There was a boy from China,
he liked to have a Chinese,
he ate it all up
in a matter of minutes.
That was the young boy from China.

Then a boy from Wales,
was running through the windy gales,
with a swish of a wand,
he ended up in a bomb!
That was the young boy of Wales.

Owain Tobin (10)
Ysgol Gymraeg Bro Ogwr, Bridgend

Cross-Country

Cross-country is what I do best,
I run like a whippet when put to the test,
Keeping in front to the same pace
By doing this I have won the race.

Up and down slopes I sometimes run,
Through puddles and mud it makes it more fun.
Both sprinting and long distance I like,
For cross-country I wear my running spikes.

No matter the weather, warm sunshine or rain,
This kind of sport I still have to train.
Around the comp schools that's where I compete
I hope, one day, I'll be a great athlete!

Calvin Richards (10)
Ysgol Gymraeg Bro Ogwr, Bridgend

Colours

Blue is the colour of the deep blue sea.
Yellow is the colour of a buzzy, buzzy bee.
Green is the colour of the mouldy seaweed.
Brown is the colour of the tiny little seeds.
Red is the colour of the sunset in the east.
Black is the colour of the ferocious beast.
These are the best colours ever!

Lauren Davies (10)
Ysgol Gymraeg Bro Ogwr, Bridgend

My Day At Longleat

I went to Longleat the other day,
Hoping to see some monkeys play,
Lions, elephants and tigers too,
They are all there, it's quite a big zoo.

On safari we would go,
Seeing the crocs and the hippos.
But of all the animals that we saw,
The seals made me laugh and scream.

But then it was time, we had to go,
The bus was waiting and the driver knew
That we'd be back again some day,
To watch those seals and monkeys play.

Darian James (9)
Ysgol Gymraeg Bro Ogwr, Bridgend

Sports

S ports is having fun
P eople getting ready to run
O ver the bar in high jump
R eady to land with a bump
T hrow your javelin high and long
S hotput started with a gong.

William Thomas (10)
Ysgol Gymraeg Bro Ogwr, Bridgend

Alone In The Snow

S kiing on the snowy mountain.
N o other people around.
O n your own in stormy weather.
W ith no sight or sound.

James Harris (10)
Ysgol Gymraeg Bro Ogwr, Bridgend

Myself

My name is Jack,
I've got an achy back,
I've lost my shoe,
I fell in goo,
But I don't complain about that.

I like to sing and dance,
I'll dance all the way to France,
I fell with glee,
But broke my knee,
And now I've lost my pants.

Bradley James Turner (10)
Ysgol Gymraeg Bro Ogwr, Bridgend

My Pizza

That pizza is mine
And I love it so much, *yum!*
'Mum, please get me some
With chicken and ham
With some pepperoni, Mum.'
I love pizza.

Pizza is awesome
And pizza is brilliant, *yum!*
Pizza is the best.

Ellis Cooper (8)
Ysgol Gymraeg Bro Ogwr, Bridgend

Thunder And Lightning

When I see the lightning
I start to count Mississippis
Which can be very frightening.

When I hear the thunder,
How close is it to this area? I wonder.

I divide my Mississippis by five
And if it's close, under my bed
I dive.

Dylan Edwards (10)
Ysgol Gymraeg Bro Ogwr, Bridgend

Friends

F riends are people you can't buy
R emember they are to play with, not to fight with
I nteresting things about each other
E veryone has a friend, not just me
N o one's left out, can you see?
D reaming of happy days
S ometimes sad, but not for long because our friendship
will always be strong!

Kate Cook (10)
Ysgol Gymraeg Bro Ogwr, Bridgend

The Chicken Burger

My burger is nice,
It's got mayonnaise on it,
It's very yummy!
It's got a brown bun,
A soft and lumpy pillow,
That is scrummy too!
Inside, there's lettuce,
Like green waves, crunchy and sweet,
Like a beautiful rose!
The chicken is last,
Wrapped in a big brown blanket,
Do you think it's lush?

Aimiee Hannah Pullen (8)
Ysgol Gymraeg Bro Ogwr, Bridgend

The Guinea Pig Kennings

Fruit eater
Pig looker
Hay sleeper
Fast runner
Human biter
Water drinker
Hutch liver
Furry creature
Grass lover
Named Barney
Very funny!

Daniel Lewis (9)
Ysgol Gymraeg Bro Ogwr, Bridgend

Dragon Of The Night

D ragon of the night
R aging through the night
A fight for his life
G oing to take place this night
O n the plains of Africa
N othing can save him tonight

O K, his life is coming to an end
F or tonight he will be slaughtered.

T he dragon in a cage
H olding him through the night
E verything quiet for his death tonight.

N o, he isn't happy
I f killing is his hobby
G et into the cage for doing it, I do
H olding him through the night
T he dragon of the night.

Luke Fletcher (10)
Ysgol Gymraeg Bro Ogwr, Bridgend

Chinese

I love barbecue
But my mum hates it a lot
And I don't get it.

Chinese is the best
She must be really weird, how?
She is losing out.

'What's for dinner, Mum?
Can we have Chinese?'
'No, no!'
'Why can't we?' Dad says.

Owen Watkin (9)
Ysgol Gymraeg Bro Ogwr, Bridgend

Faithful Pal

He is always pleased to see me,
He never growls or barks
Unless it is a stranger
Or he is playing in the park.
He has got a waggy tail
And very sad brown eyes,
And when he wants a walk
In the hallway he lies.
He's black from his nose
To the tip of his tail,
And his name is Ebony
He's my faithful pal.

Yasmine Saman (10)
Ysgol Gymraeg Bro Ogwr, Bridgend

Most Haunted

Me and my parents are never daunted,
because we love watching TV's 'Most Haunted'.
The ghosts and mediums we just love.
The mediums and people that they try to shove.
There's Karl, Yvette, Stuart and Cath
leading us on the ghostly path.
We think it is wonderful and spooky, you see.
Try and watch it, you'll see.
It's better than 'Dead Famous', we agree.

Lisa Whittaker (9)
Ysgol Gymraeg Bro Ogwr, Bridgend

Wicked Wine Gums - Haiku

Oh how I love these
Scrummy, yummy to eat, yum!
Roll up, chewy sweets.

Tyler Richards (9)
Ysgol Gymraeg Bro Ogwr, Bridgend

Dogs In Togs

Dogs in togs
Are playing on the logs.
They come in different breeds,
They grow like seeds,
And you put them on leads.
Dogs are loyal
And guard the royals.
They have cute paws
And like to use their claws.
They like to eat,
Especially their meat.
They hate cats
And chew rats.
Some dogs like to sit by the fire,
With a bit of music from the choir.

Ffion Edwards (9)
Ysgol Gymraeg Bro Ogwr, Bridgend

Guinea Minnie

'Guinea Mini, what have you done?'
'I've been to Gregg's and had a bun!'
'Guinea Mini, where have you been?'
'I've been to London to see the Queen!'
'Guinea Mini, what have you got?'
'I've got a bean from the Queen!'
'Guinea Mini, what's wrong?'
'I haven't got long!'
'Guinea Mini, what's wrong?'
'Dinner, dinner! Well, I want dinner and when
I come back I'll
Be a
Winner!'

Elin Crockett (9)
Ysgol Gymraeg Bro Ogwr, Bridgend

Make-Believe

Whoever said trolls looked like dolls
And witches and wizards are true?
Scary fire-breathing dragons,
And red-eyed monster demons,
People wearing invisible cloaks
And little green men and fairy folk,
The world of Harry Potter walking and talking,
Tooth fairies, aliens, Loch Ness monster, pixies
And forests full of talking trees!
Whoever said they were true?
They are all make-believe,
Are you?

Elin Angharad Morgan (11)
Ysgol Gymraeg Bro Ogwr, Bridgend

My Computer

Me	'It's my turn now.'
Brother	'It's still my turn because Mam said half an hour!'
Me	'Half an hour has been ages.'
Brother	'No, it hasn't.'
Me	'Yes, it has, trust me.'
Brother	'I am sitting here all day.'
Me	'No, you are not.'
Brother	'Yes I am.'
Me	'I'm going to tell Mam on you . . . *owww!* Mam!'

Catherine Booth (9)
Ysgol Gymraeg Bro Ogwr, Bridgend

Delicious Fish - Haiku

Yummy, lovely fish
Gift-wrapped in golden batter
It's ready to eat!

Lauren Elizabeth Davies
Ysgol Gymraeg Bro Ogwr, Bridgend

A Monkey's Banana

It's a yellow boat,
Except it doesn't float
Up in a banana tree.

It's nice and ripe,
Round like a pipe,
How lucky we are to have one of these.
They're full of flavour,
They do us a favour,
Helping us keep nice and healthy!

Catrin Hâf Jones (9)
Ysgol Gymraeg Bro Ogwr, Bridgend

My Rabbit

I have a pet called Patch,
On his cage there's a latch,
He lives in a hutch,
I love him very much.

He's a pest,
But the best,
My adorable hunny bunny,
He likes to suck a dummy.

Eilidh Meldrum (9)
Ysgol Gymraeg Bro Ogwr, Bridgend

My Pet Dog

My pet dog is hilarious,
He makes me laugh all night,
He's really fast and fluffy and furry,
When I race him, he is always the first.

Rhiannon Kemp (9)
Ysgol Gymraeg Bro Ogwr, Bridgend

Monkey Business

Will you think I was mad,
Or possibly sad,
If I tell you that I have a monkey
Who is really quite funky?
He lives in a cupboard,
And is known as Mother Hubbard
His favourite dish
Is fillets of fish,
He enjoys a glass of Chardonnay
Each Saturday.
My monkey is great,
He's my best mate.

Iona Elizabeth Sayer (11)
Ysgol Gymraeg Bro Ogwr, Bridgend

The Fairy

There once was a fairy called Mary
Who was really hairy
She loved to fly up in the sky
But she ate a lot of pies
And told a lot of lies
She travelled around the world
But she didn't like to twirl
That is the hairy fairy called Mary.

Rebecca Leigh Howells (11)
Ysgol Gymraeg Bro Ogwr, Bridgend

Scrumptious Chicken - Haiku

Lovely to eat now
It's cool and brown, delicious:
Chicken is scrumptious.

Peter Mayne (9)
Ysgol Gymraeg Bro Ogwr, Bridgend

The Ugly Dog

There once was an ugly dog,
Who got lost in the fog,
When he come home,
He was given a bone,
Tucked him in tight,
Shut off the light,
And hoped that he was alright.

Hannah-May Maddern (10)
Ysgol Gymraeg Bro Ogwr, Bridgend

Hot Dogs

Love me to eat,
Eat me, love me always
You can eat me girls.

They look like brown bones
On the flaming barbecue
That you want to eat.

Keighley Jade Jones (9)
Ysgol Gymraeg Bro Ogwr, Bridgend

Fairyland

In the misty full moon,
By the stream, fairies come,
Tap their feet to the fairy beat,
Then off they go to a different scene.
Where they go it's up to them.

Kayleigh Rose Leach (11)
Ysgol Gymraeg Bro Ogwr, Bridgend

Harry, Dragon And The Pond

One day a young boy called Harry,
Met a dragon going his way,
With a swish of his wand,
They fell into a pond,
And woke up in Cardiff Bay.

They came out all muddy and wet,
And also slightly confused,
With a wave of his wand,
Harry started to bond,
With a girl on ITV News.

The young girl's name was Mary,
And they both were madly in love,
But as he was waving his wand,
To go back to the pond,
Mary ended up flying above.

So Harry tried again,
Waving his useless wand,
As Harry and the dragon disappeared,
Everyone thought it was very weird,
For them to be diving into a pond.

Calum Thompson (10)
Ysgol Gymraeg Bro Ogwr, Bridgend

Rugby Mad

The day has come for Wales vs England.
It's time to cheer and chant,
Dad for England and me for Wales,
The whistle blows, Wales score a *try!*
And Dad cries in his beer.
'Don't worry, Dad, you'll get your chance
Just not this year!'

William Emlyn Booth (10)
Ysgol Gymraeg Bro Ogwr, Bridgend

The Hairy Fairy

I met a fairy called Mary,
She was not scary but hairy,
She had wide eyes and feet, size nines,
And she was not normal for a fairy of her kind.

She grew taller than the others
And was laughed at by all of her brothers,
But what they didn't know
Was that she was the princess of all the land's snow.

When it snows at night
She reveals her true glow and smiles for hours
She floats up high, up into the sky
And feels better than all of the others.

If only they knew what happened at night -
That she turned into a glittering goddess of light.

True beauty lies within.

Rachelle June Morris (11)
Ysgol Gymraeg Bro Ogwr, Bridgend

Izzy The Fairy

There was a fairy called Izzy
Who flew until she was dizzy
She bought a clock
It went tick-tock
And that was the fairy called Izzy.

Jessica Anne Evans (11)
Ysgol Gymraeg Bro Ogwr, Bridgend

The Musical Cat

There was a cat who liked to wear hats
And play music with a *tap, tap, tap.*
He would tap on a fence and tap on a bin
Looking around with a cheeky grin.
His friends had said that he was the best doing the tap,
But there were always people shouting 'Shut up!'
He would tap all night and tap all day,
This was the cat who liked to play the *tap, tap, tap*
With his colourful hat.

Zak Harries
Ysgol Gymraeg Bro Ogwr, Bridgend

Disney

D is for dinosaurs in the land before time
I is for the 'Incredibles' battling against crime
S is for Sinbad sailing the seven seas
N is for Nemo swimming wherever he feels
E is for the Emperor in his new groove
Y is for young Peter Pan with something to prove.

Disney means lots of things to both young and old
As these wonderful fairy tales are so often retold.

Geraint Watkin
Ysgol Gymraeg Bro Ogwr, Bridgend

Mary The Fairy

There was a fairy named Mary
She was very hairy
With a wave of a wand
She ended up in a pond
That was the hairy fairy, Mary.

Rhiannon Megan Cichocki (11)
Ysgol Gymraeg Bro Ogwr, Bridgend

A Unicorn

There was a unicorn called Roxy
The boys thought she was foxy
She was pink and white
And she never gave you a fright.

She was afraid of the dark
But she liked the light
Roxy was very friendly
And she never used to bite.

That was the foxy Roxy.

Stephanie Cichocki (11)
Ysgol Gymraeg Bro Ogwr, Bridgend

Kaka

There was a boy called Kaka,
He liked to do the Haka,

He loved to watch Laka Taka,
He lived in Mirocataka,

He used to be in the war,
But he saw a boy get clawed,

And that's the boy Kaka,
Who liked to do the Haka.

Morgan Emanuel (11)
Ysgol Gymraeg Bro Ogwr, Bridgend